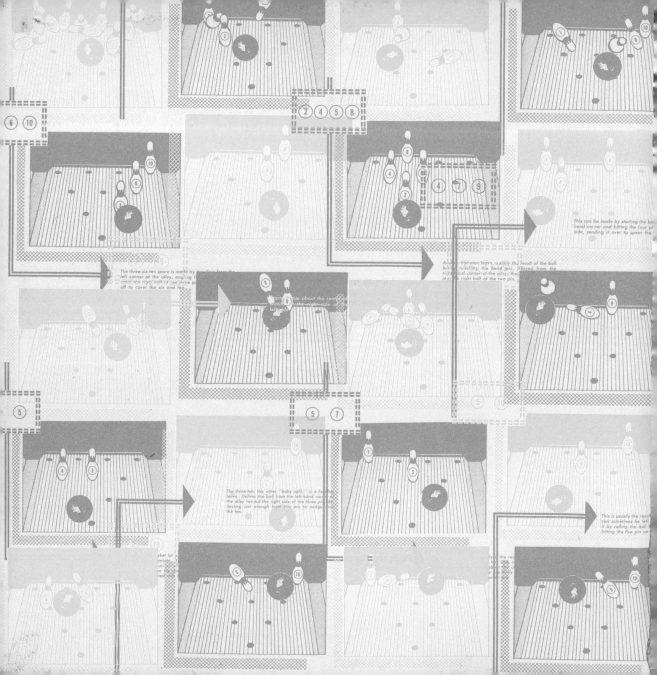

BOWLED OVER

bowled

A ROLL DOWN MEMORY LANE

*by Gideon Bosker
and Bianca Lenček-Bosker*

over

CHRONICLE BOOKS
SAN FRANCISCO

TO LENA LENČEK
who has bowled us over with love, wisdom, and intelligence

Photographs and illustrations courtesy **THE INTERNATIONAL BOWLING MUSEUM AND HALL OF FAME**, except: **pp. 2 – 3:** Illustration from *Bowling Secrets of the Pros*, edited by George Sullivan, drawings by Dom Lupo, Doubleday & Company, Inc., 1968. **p. 4:** Illustration from *Bowling Secrets of the Pros*, edited by George Sullivan, drawings by Dom Lupo, Doubleday & Company, Inc., 1968. **p. 52:** Illustration from *Bowling Secrets of the Pros*, edited by George Sullivan, drawings by Dom Lupo, Doubleday & Company, Inc., 1968. **p. 58:** Illustration from Brunswick catalog 1972/73. **p. 59:** Illustration from *Bowling*, by Joan L. Martin, Wm. C. Brown Company Publishers, 1966. **pp. 60 – 61:** Illustration from *Bowling for Boys and Girls*, by John J. Archibald, Follett Publishing Company, 1963. **p. 63:** Inset illustration from *How to Improve Your Bowling*, Athletic Institute, no date. **p. 70:** Illustration from *Bowling for Boys and Girls*, by John J. Archibald, Follett Publishing Company, 1963. **p. 77:** Illustration from *Bowling for Boys and Girls*, by John J. Archibald, Follett Publishing Company, 1963. **pp. 78 – 79:** Illustrations from Brunswick catalog 1971/72 and Brunswick catalog 1972/73. **pp. 84 – 85:** Illustration from *Bowling*, by Joan L. Martin, Wm. C. Brown Company Publishers, 1966. **p. 98:** Illustration from Mother Jones Bowlsheviks, 1999. **p. 109:** Photograph by Bettman/Corbis, 1947. **p. 115:** Illustration from *Bowling for Boys and Girls*, by John J. Archibald, Follett Publishing Company, 1963. **p. 124:** Photograph by Jeffery Walls, 2001. **Endpapers:** Illustrations from *Bowling to Win*, by Buzz Fazio, Grosset & Dunlap, Inc., 1955.

Every effort has been made to trace the ownership of all copyrighted material included in this volume. Any errors that may have occured are inadvertent and will be corrected in subsequent editions, provided notification is sent to the publisher.

Library of Congress Cataloging-in-Publication Data available.

ISBN: 0-8118-3382-8

Manufactured in China

Book and cover design by Benjamin Shaykin

Distributed in Canada by
Raincoast Books
9050 Shaughnessy Street
Vancouver, British Columbia V6P 6E5

10 9 8 7 6 5 4 3 2 1

Chronicle Books LLC
85 Second Street
San Francisco, California 94105
www.chroniclebooks.com

EACH PIN IS
REGISTERED*

CONTENTS

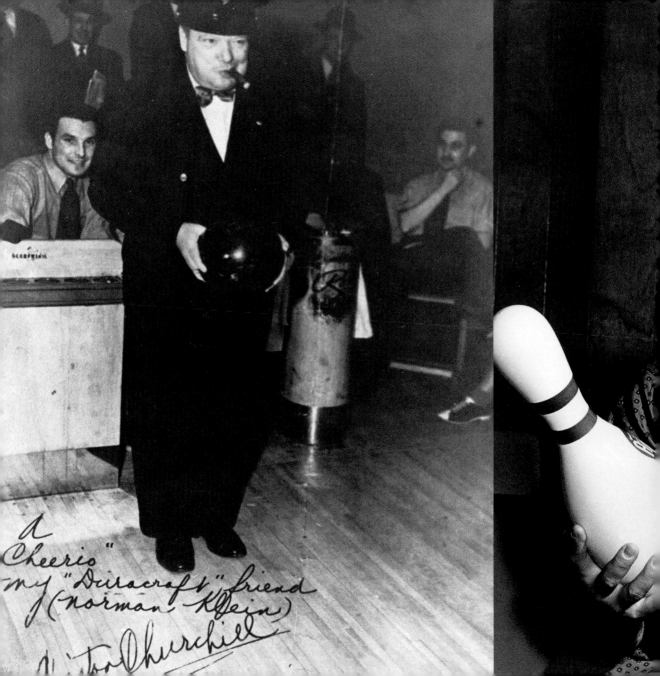

A "Cheerio" my "Duracraft" friend (Norman Klein) Winston Churchill

Right Down My Alley

Since my days growing up outside Chicago I've been an avid bowler. Along with my passion for Oreo cookies, the Ravinia music festival, golden-arched McDonald's restaurants, and the Chicago Cubs, my weekly pilgrimages to the alleys defined the high points of my early adolescence. The crackle, snap, and thunder of pins being hit squarely by gleaming black orbs, followed by the thud of the ball against the Naugahyde backdrop at the end of the lane, is permanently etched in my acoustic memory. So is the swooshing of the ball as it popped through the ball return, and the sometimes gleeful,

sometimes exasperating shouts of "Strike!" or "All right!" or "Darn it!" above the din of wood striking wood. I remember the two-tone watermelon-and-red bowling shoes I rented, and the unpleasant odors wafting from the shoe-rental stall. During those years, the balls my friends and I used were anything but glamorous. Black was the standard color for the "house balls" that were our lot. We could always spot the bowling aficionados, because they arrived with multicolored bags, from which they plucked multicolored Mineralite balls that were all the rage. I remember walking the six blocks to the Howard Bowl in Chicago where my friends and I would bowl a round of four or five games. And when I couldn't make it to the alley, there was always a Saturday afternoon bowling tournament to watch on my family's black-and-white TV: short guys with butch-waxed hair cut boot-camp style, wearing floppy shirts and launching black balls at ivory-white pins that, if hit just right, scattered as if into oblivion.

It's no coincidence that I became smitten with the game in the "City of Big Shoulders," where working-class immigrants powered the

postwar industrial engine just as they did in other heartland outposts such as Detroit, Cleveland, and St. Louis. What I learned during my initiation into the sport was that the modern game of bowling originated in the factory, was popularized by the factory, and projected the ethos and acoustic ambience of the factory. From the dull roar, thunderous claps, and mechanical clang-jangle of automated pinsetters to the arrangement of the alleys, with their clean geometry and mechanics reminiscent of a conveyor-belt line, bowling was a workingman's game that put a premium on precision, piecework, and team play. Here was a recreational setting where the sound of machines prevailed over the sound of human voices, and where the body's movements were governed by a single imperative—to hook a rolling sphere made of hard rubber into the 1-3 pin pocket and knock ten pins to the floor.

Bowled Over: A Roll Down Memory Lane harks back to that earlier era, when bowling champ Don Carter was as much of a household name as Dick Clark. Today's retro trendsetters and high-fashion houses have embraced the game's aesthetic, with their bowling-inspired shoes, bags, shirts, and accessories. Collectors are witnessing skyrocketing prices for vintage bowling shirts, and manufacturers have started making reproductions. But fashion trends aside, bowling is still with us, with hundreds of leagues proliferating from Bakersfield to Baltimore. Once the most watched sport in America, bowling is now—with an estimated 70 million participants—the one most played. The game is not only a family pastime and everyman sport but also a disco-pop indulgence for the hip, the young, and the restless. The alleys are alive with rock music, and black lights have turned "cosmic bowling" into a theater of flying pins and glimmering balls careening down invisible floors.

—Gideon Bosker   **13**

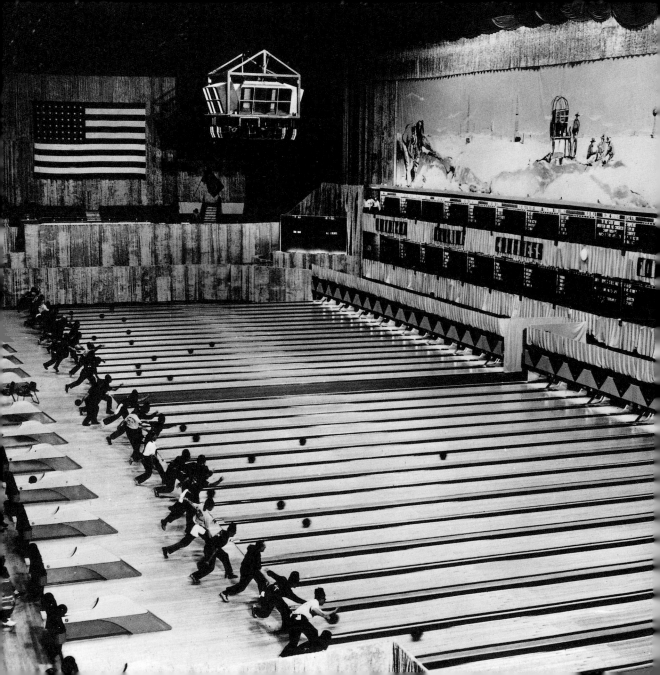

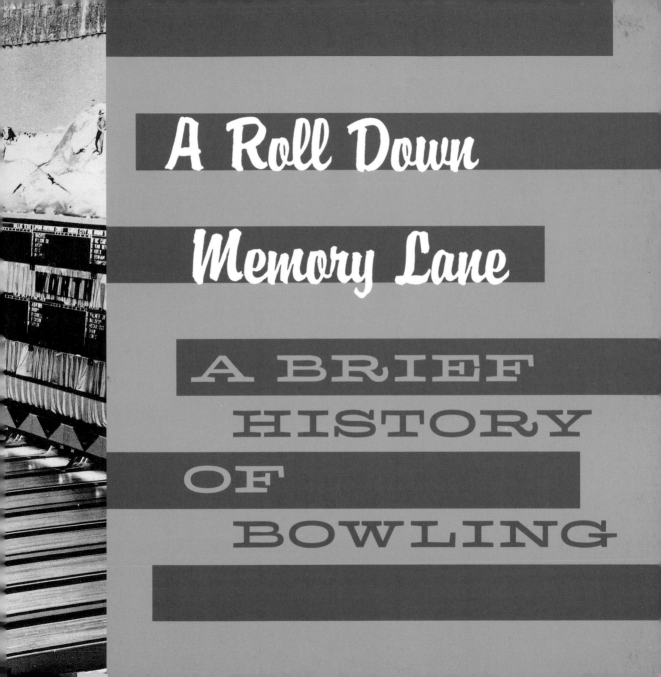

A Roll Down Memory Lane

A BRIEF HISTORY OF BOWLING

LONG BEFORE BOWLING CHAMP DON CARTER'S locked-elbow, free-shoulder approach revolutionized the game in the 1950s, humans were rolling balls at standing objects. In fact, grisly legends testify to early bowling practices, such as those of the ancient Indo-European tribes of the vast Asiatic steppes, who bowled at upright thighbones with the skulls of vanquished enemies, using the eye and nose sockets for thumb and finger grips. And, in the 1930s, British archaeologist Sir Flinders Petrie discovered a collection of implements in a child's grave in Egypt dating to 5200 B.C. that may be evidence of a crude form of bowling.

The English game of "bowling on the green" originated in the late thirteenth century, allegedly on Crown Greene in Southampton, where it is played to this day. By 1366 the game had taken such a hold of the populace that King Edward III felt compelled to outlaw it to keep his troops focused on archery, which, unlike bowling, had important military value. Henry VIII, however, was obsessed with the game and contrived to make it an exclusive "sport of kings," decreeing the game off-limits to the poor. But despite the best royal efforts at restrictive legislation, the British passion for the sport continued to thrive underground. Finally, in 1845, the British crown gave up the fight for an exclusively aristocratic monopoly on the game and granted the British people the right to play "bowls" to their hearts' content.

Bowling as we know it today has its origins in the similar game of ninepins that was played more than four centuries ago in Germany and Holland. Martin Luther, for example, was so fond of this game he built a private "rink" for himself and his family. Today, the game in Germany is played, as it was then, with nine pins arranged in a diamond formation. Called *Kegelspiel* (bowlers in Germany are referred to as "keglers"), the game was brought to America by early Dutch settlers in New York.

But it was the British variant of "Crown Green" or "Lawn Bowling" that first captured the American imagination in the early 1600s. The first facility was established in 1733, in New York's Bowling Green Park. To this day the small plot on which the original gaming ground stood is still called "Bowling Green." Although some looked to the game as a distinguished, genteel pastime, in the early nineteenth century it was surrounded by so much gambling and racketeering that bowling was outlawed in New York, Connecticut, and Massachusetts. An 1841 Connecticut statute made it illegal to maintain "any ninepin lanes," but bowling enthusiasts evaded these laws simply by adding a tenth pin and changing the configuration from a diamond to a triangle. The "new" game mushroomed in popularity, and by the 1860s, basement rooms for playing tenpins lined every block along Broadway from Fulton to 14th Street. Smitten by the tenpin craze, captains of industry installed bowling lanes in their mansions from the Hudson Valley to Long Island.

By the late nineteenth century, bowling had spread as far west as Illinois and Ohio. Although many wealthy folks enjoyed bowling in private gentlemen's clubs, estate lanes, or garden lanes, bowling continued to be more closely linked with the central institution of working-class immigrant social life—the saloon. In fact, "bowling saloons" were the primary means by which the game was introduced to the masses. While the name for the establishment suggests a certain air of refinement, the setting was far from glamorous. Bowling by the beginning of the twentieth century was part and parcel of the dreary recreational repertoire of the poor that included beer drinking, tobacco chewing, and gambling in depressing, airless dives. With one or two lanes each, saloons were nothing more than damp, dimly illuminated, poorly ventilated basements. No respectable man, woman, or child would even consider entering such a place.

In this formative period, the game of bowling was a ragtag, nonstandardized affair with details like weights of balls and pin dimensions varying by region and even

19

by lane or saloon. In 1875, New Yorkers attempting to standardize the game scored their first success. Twenty-seven delegates from nine Manhattan and Brooklyn bowling clubs banded together to form the National Bowling Association. They began by setting the distance from the foul line to the head pin at 60 feet and standardizing pin dimensions. Two decades later, restaurateur-cum-bowling champion Joe Thum pulled together representatives of the various regional bowling clubs, forming the American Bowling Congress and further refining the game. Once standardized, national bowling competitions could be launched.

As national organizations blossomed and the game's popularity continued to grow, two technological breakthroughs set the stage for massive growth. In 1905, the

first rubber ball, the "Evertrue," was introduced. By 1914, the Brunswick Corporation was successfully promoting the Mineralite ball, which, with its patented "mysterious rubber compound," became bowling's signature weapon. Mechanization also enabled bowling to take a giant step forward. The first commercial installation of an automatic pinspotter (a device for resetting pins) was made in Michigan in 1951, and within a few years, automation had taken hold. No longer did proprietors have to rely on a corps of unruly "pinboys" to keep the games going. A few higher-paid mechanics could do the job of setting up numerous lanes more efficiently with fewer man-hours each day.

Eventually, grace, elegance, and finesse took over not only the game, but also the alleys. Influenced by the streamlined, modernist aesthetic that prevailed from the 1930s through the 1950s, bowling establishments, especially in California, evolved into sumptuous recreational outposts. Bowling alleys sparkled with the glitter and flash of mid-century modern design, which was evident in cocktail bars and restaurants, as well as in the kidney-shaped sofas, Eames easy chairs, and plush carpets which muted the nonstop crack and splatter of balls against pins at the end of fifty maple-skinned lanes. The game accelerated into high gear with the introduction of industrial bowling leagues and aggressive marketing campaigns aiming to make bowling a family sport.

When television began experimenting with broadcasting bowling in the 1950s, the game's popularity grew exponentially. NBC pioneered network coverage with *Championship Bowling*, paving the way for shows such as *Make That Spare*, *Celebrity Bowling*, *Jackpot Bowling*, and *Bowling for Dollars*. By the end of the decade, however, interest in bowling began to lag, perhaps due to overexposure and oversaturation, poor media presentation, or a general economic "bust."

But elsewhere bowling became wildly popular. In the 1970s, the sport became so popular in Japan that journalists called it "an addiction second only to golf." During

STOCK
ESS
B. A.
031

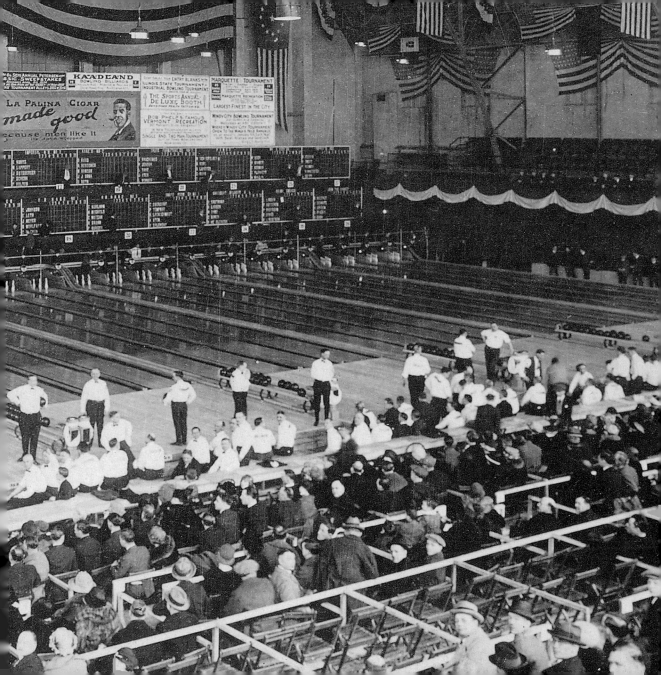

the 1970s and 1980s, Japan possessed the second-largest bowling population after the United States, and it still boasts the world's largest bowling alley—Tokyo's 252-lane World Lanes. The World Lanes' seven-story building—with two more floors underground—remains the world's largest bowling facility. The alley's kitchen prepares four thousand meals a day, and its shops are packed. In 1973, on an average day, ten thousand bowlers played the lanes; the figure jumped to twice or three times that on holidays.

Meanwhile, the Pro Bowlers Tour became a hugely popular part of ABC sports broadcasting, in part thanks to charismatic bowling pros who wowed television audiences with their staggering precision and fierce competitive spirit. When the Professional Bowler's Association (PBA) was joined later by telecasts of the Ladies Pro Bowlers Tour, millions of Americans witnessed and became interested in the sport.

Organized competitive leagues remain the foundation of bowling in the United States. However, more than 70 percent of leagues today consist of people of mixed skills, making for a more relaxed level of competition. Also, evenings of "organized open" play, such as Saturday night "rock and bowl" and "cosmic bowling" events, are growing in importance to bowling-alley proprietors throughout the country. Although we may not have the bowling celebrities and heroes we had in the 1950s and 1960s, a hundred million people in more than ninety countries worldwide enjoy bowling. The fashionable flourishes, flashing lights, Day-Glo bowling balls, and rock music that energize cosmic bowling on non-league nights testify that the game has come a long way from the skull-bowlers and filthy saloons of yore.

The Automatic

Fanatic

BOWLING ENTERS THE MACHINE AGE

GOING AUTOMATIC PUT BOWLING IN A NEW LEAGUE—IT CATAPULTED

the sport into a full-fledged mainstream American pastime with all the bells and whistles of assembly-line recreation and machine-age aesthetics. No other sport was as influenced by the introduction of mechanization as was bowling. Machines in the bowling arena meant more people could be accommodated more efficiently, the game could move at a much brisker pace, and alley operations could be more profitable.

Equip your alleys with MAGIC

"Magic" Bowling Equipment is the answer to every bowling proprietor's dreams. It combines beauty with low upkeep and a lifetime of service. Made of lustrous, stainless steel tubing, "Magic" ball returns are noiseless and never need refinishing to keep their gleaming appearance. The "Magic" ball retarder is a masterpiece of engineering skill. Nothing to wear out, nothing to go wrong, it stops all balls safelyand gently without loops or traps and never allows the ball to roll back onto the return.

Automation proceeded gradually and incrementally. Between 1939 and 1950, even as the game was moving toward greater mechanization of pinsetting, it still relied on pinboys to provide the nuts-and-bolts technical support. By 1942, most pinboys had become accustomed to using some kind of mechanical device to reset pins. The standard unit was a metal contraption that was manually loaded with pins, lowered into position, and then raised out of the way of the ball. Although it marked an improvement by helping accelerate the pace of the game, the pinsetter still required the services of pinboys, who ultimately controlled the speed of the game and, in many cases, the enjoyment of its participants.

In 1946, the American Machine and Foundry Company launched the first automated pinsetter. Serious glitches, however, prevented the rapid and widespread adoption of the device. The machine was not only a behemoth, weighing in at more than two tons; it was also unpredictable in its ability to reset pins, and required constant recalibration and servicing. It took almost five years to produce an automated pinspotter that could reset pins flawlessly without human intervention. In 1952, the first refined, fully operational system was installed at the sixteen-lane Farragut Pool

HYDRO-PNEUMATIC PIN SPOTTER READY!

PERFECTED, TIME-TESTED

WHY ADVERTISE for PIN BOYS? WITH A NEW MEAD PIN SPOTTER —they'll be waiting in line!

Simple—easily installed

Lanes in Brooklyn, New York. Despite the costs associated with the new technology, lane owners breathed a sigh of relief at not having to hire and manage unruly pinboys.

The first automatic fanatics with the vision to install automated pinspotters saw their volume of customers—and their profits—increase dramatically. The Fairview Bowling Center, one of the first establishments in Cleveland to employ the new AMF product, advertised in 1954: "The AMF machine picks and returns the ball . . . sets up the pins . . . clears the lanes of deadwood . . . Seeing is believing . . . so come in and see for yourself." And once customers did so, they saw for themselves that the marriage between the machine and the bowling ball was here to stay.

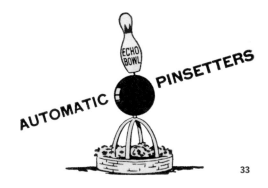

AUTOMATIC PINSETTERS

ECHO BOWL

Considering how many grimy fingers make their way into a house ball, one can only be grateful to the genius who invented the revolutionary sanitary blown-air hand-and-ball dryer sometime in 1956. Brunswick, the manufacturer, touted the Electric-Aire Hand Dryer as an item "bowlers have long awaited and will fully appreciate" and claimed that "seasoned authorities who have participated in FIELD TESTS recommend 'THE BOWL-AIR'

hand and ball dryer, because it eliminates CHALK-GERM INFESTED HAND TOWELS and gives your bowler that dry hand and ball which he needs for better control to improve his game." In addition, this gizmo was promoted as not only completely eliminating moisture in finger holes (a frequent cause for dropped balls), but as being "highly accepted by medical authorities throughout the nation."

WHAT EVERY
BOWLER NEEDS
SEE-SAW BALL CLEANER

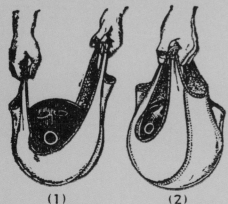

(1)   (2)

An innovation to clean, carry and protect your bowling ball. To clean the ball you work back and forth in a "see-saw" action, as in figure 1. Figure 2 illustrates how it carries the ball. Used in your regular bag, to keep your ball clean and free from contacting your shoes.

No. A69—Plus 15c Postage—No Tax
Each 75c

No. A60—1 pint Ball-Rite Cleaner and Polisher (removes dirt rings). Each 55c

No. A61—1 quart Ball-Rite Cleaner and Polisher (removes dirt rings). Each 90c

A Roll Down

Architecture Alley

THE
GAME
GOES
GLEAM

SPIT-SHINED FLOORS, NEON SIGNAGE, AND the shine of molded plastic: these were the motifs that characterized bowling-alley design during the "Age of Gleam" between 1945 and 1960. In the barroom setting, lanes were relegated to poorly illuminated basements, side rooms, and makeshift sheds where little attention was paid to anything beyond the basics: a hard floor, a wooden ball, and ten wooden pins. More often than not, bowling lanes had few redeeming decorative or architectural features. The modern mid-century bowling alley, with its sweeping lines, muted acoustics, and overhead projections of score sheets—not to mention children's playrooms—had come a long way from the tawdry speakeasy environments of bowling saloons.

During prohibition, alleys began cleaning up their acts in an effort to transform bowling's sullied reputation and lure families into their establishments. Owners made simple aesthetic modifications, such as splashing colored paint on the walls and masking unsightly pipes and water drains with curtains or plaster. Others went further and equipped their alleys with soundproofing, overhead lighting, and spectator seating. With spruced-up alleys, it's no wonder Americans fell in love with bowling: from 1946 to 1964, the number of bowlers more than doubled, to nearly 40 million players.

From an architectural perspective, bowling alleys designed between the late 1940s and early 1960s, the zenith of the sport's popularity, were jet-age expressions of a sleek, curvilinear, no-colors-or-shapes-barred

aesthetic. Many alleys featured detailed murals chronicling American sporting life, the space age, or the Wild West. In March 1958, *Life* magazine noted that the American bowling alley, "once stuck shamefacedly in a back-street basement," had finally acquired a "stunning elegance and had bloomed into an all-purpose pleasure palace offering variety in entertainment and luxury. Its façades have the glitter of a Hollywood nightclub. Its deep-carpeted lobbies are lined with restaurants, cocktail lounges, billiard and beauty parlors."

Some proprietors pulled out all the stops to dazzle their customers. Suburban Lanes, in Buffalo, featured built-in "wall cribs," a state-of-the-art outdoor barbecue patio, and a swimming pool. According to promotional materials, Frank Esposito called his forty-two-lane bowling center in Paramus, New Jersey, "a country club open to the public." It featured "spiffy wall-to-wall carpet, a cozy cocktail bar, a diner with foot-longs to die for, and a nursery with closed-circuit TV, so Mom could bowl and watch Junior at the same time." Thus, the bowling alley was on its way toward becoming an architectural icon.

Strachota-●●●●, Inc.
24 - Bowling Lanes - 24
Cocktail Lounge - Restaurant
None Finer Anywhere

IMPERIAL L...

48 LANES

FOR OPEN PLAY   •   FOR

NES

EAGUE PLAY

Havin' a Ball

FROM ROCK TO RUBBER AND BEYOND

IF YOU ASKED BOWLERS AT YOUR LOCAL ALLEY TO MAKE
a strike with, say, a crude round stone, they would most likely stare at you
in disbelief or alarm, or both. But the fact is, the history of the bowling ball is
nothing less than a "rock of ages" story with a twist. Considering all the technological advances and refinements that have gone into the development of today's pol-
ished, multilayered bowling ball, who would believe that a crude rock was its
great-granddaddy? Yet it seems that when bowling began in medieval Germany,
every God-fearing peasant proved his faith by rolling rocks at his club, or *Kegel*, set
up in the parish churchyard. Admittedly, it took a lot of faith—or ale—to see a hea-
then lurking in every Kegel, but even with a rock ball, one could still bowl well enough
to knock down a few pins, and that, after all, was the bottom line.

As the game moved from the churchyard to the tavern, the solitary wooden
cudgel morphed into multiple pins, and the rolling stone was replaced by a wooden
one. By the eleventh century A.D. balls made of wood were standard. It wasn't until
the 20th century that the first rubber ball was introduced as a novelty. Under the
brand name "Evertrue," it went into mass production in 1914. The manufacturer
claimed that its "mysterious rubber compound," dubbed mineralite, would revolution-
ize the game. And indeed, the new spheres so effectively knocked down wooden
pins—and so dramatically reduced the noise level in alleys—that they quickly outsold
the wooden competition. The invention of mineralite also helped establish the
Brunswick Corporation as the leading purveyor of supplies for the game.

The preeminence of rubber, however, lasted only 50 years before the quest for
the perfect bowling ball resumed. Working with physicists and chemists, bowling ball
designers studied the effects of a player's handedness (right or left) and quality of
release (spin, speed, loft, direction) on the ball's performance, as well as the types
of lane surfaces a bowler was likely to encounter.

When you purchase a bowling ball, an experienced professional will utilize this measuring device to determine the precise size of thumb and finger holes you require.

A bowling ball is not a solid sphere, but a complex, layered construction composed of a core and a coverstock, each made of any number of materials, prepared and "finished" in a variety of ways and arranged in carefully calibrated configurations. The shape of the core also contributes to the dynamic properties of the ball. The choices in coverstock treatments extend to materials, their preparation (sanding, polishing), and their condition. Finally, the position of the finger holes and the orientation of the core determine the balance, making the ball cover-heavy or center-heavy. As expert bowlers and ball drillers discovered by trial and error, the performance of a ball can be further modified by judicious placement of finger holes and even by the addition of extra holes.

The traditional twentieth-century ball had a hard rubber shell filled with some lighter material. Late twentieth-century design kept this basic anatomy intact, but experimented with an array of space-age materials. Beginning in the 1960s, major changes were made in the coverstock material and treatment, generally involving sanding and polishing. As new substances were developed for the automotive, space, and defense industries, bowling manufacturers experimented with various kinds of

Big Roller
$35.95

Grabber, Blue
$29.95

Grabber, Black
$26.95

Lolli-pop, Grape
$29.95

Lolli-pop, Blueberry
$29.95

Lady Grabber
$29.95

Black Beauty
$21.95

Starfire II
$24.95

Crown Jewel, Blue
$23.95

Figure 4—Three Types of Balls

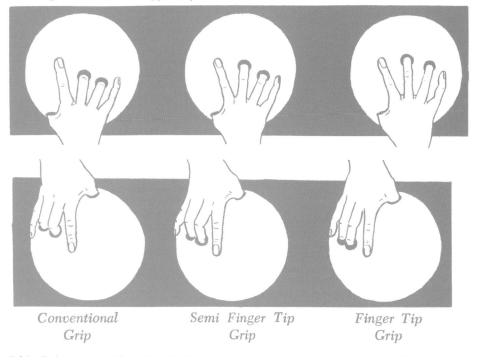

Conventional   Semi Finger Tip   Finger Tip
Grip   Grip   Grip

"skins" that ranged from hard rubber and plastic to urethane and resin. Where other areas of modern consumer culture led, bowling followed, equally seduced by the allure of synthetics: plastics, or polyesters, in the 1960s; urethane in the 1980s; and reactive resins in the 1990s.

However, as the "reactive" balls aged, their surface tended to absorb the oils from the wooden floors, producing an erratic drag in the sphere's progress along the alley, causing it to wobble, swerve, or spin unpredictably. Brunswick's Quantum ball, developed in the mid-1990s, was coated with a "proactive" textured resin allowing the ball to track evenly and "grip" the floor regardless of conditions. This textured exterior had the additional advantage of protecting the ball from wear and tear.

Important as the synergy between alley surfacing, traction, and coating properties may be, when it comes to bowling balls, it's what's on the inside that counts. A solid ceramic core enhances a ball's force because all of the energy is transferred from

IN FITTING YOUR BOWLING BALL,

check the span between the thumb and finger holes. If your fingers are stretched between the holes and cannot be fully inserted (left), the span is too wide. If your fingers are cramped between the holes, forcing your hand to curve (center), the span is too narrow. If your fingers are comfortable when properly inserted in the holes and a pencil fits between your palm and the ball (right), the span is correct.

the ball directly to the pins so that none of the ball's energy is reabsorbed by the core. In contrast, "millable" or "alloy" composite ceramic cores absorb energy and transfer it directly to the pins, producing the greatest wallop for the roll.

When it comes to weight, the heaviest ball is not the biggest one. All bowling balls are the same size: 8.59 inches in diameter. Weight, indicated by the number written on the ball's exterior, is determined by the material used in the core, which could be anything from ceramic, the lightest, to barium, the heaviest. Most balls range in weight from six to sixteen pounds. The heavier the ball, the more momentum it generates and the more force it imparts upon hitting the pins.

For once-in-a-blue-moon bowlers who just want to go out and bowl for fun, being fitted with a ball that is just right for their particular hand size and strength is not critical. Ideally, though, all bowlers would have a customized ball with holes (for thumb, middle, and ring fingers) drilled to accommodate the dimensions of their hand. Frequent bowlers need balls fit to their individualized grip, and serious bowlers usually purchase one or more custom-fitted balls, because using an ill-fitting "house ball" would cause them to compensate one way or the other on each roll, which could lead to blisters, swollen fingers and knuckles, and pulled muscles.

It is critical to know which balls will sharpen one's game, but it is just as important to know which of these rolling spheres will give the best laugh. A number of novelty balls were manufactured over the years that injected alley attitude into play. Manufacturers produced tie-dyed balls; glitter balls; balls that look like eyeballs, billiard balls, soccerballs; and Lucite balls embedded with bizarre objects, ranging from skulls to flowers to bowling pins to sea urchins. You want it, you can get it.

Bowlers—Sponsors—Spectators!

"A hit with bowlers? You bet," says an enthusiastic Tel-E-Score establishment. "Our main attraction," says another. These typical comments indicate the real showmanship and outstanding advantages in the action of Brunswick Tel-E-Scores now featured by successful operators the nation over. And there's a real profit picture too, because of the extra lines of play Tel-E-Scores promote.

Provides Play-By-Play Scores

Spotlight your establishment and dramatize the game by providing "play-by-play" scores visible to spectators and bowlers alike. Remember . . . baseball without the box score would be no fun. Tel-E-Score answers that question for bowling fans the first time in bowling's history. See your Brunswick Representative or write your nearest Brunswick Branch Office for complete details. Centennial Tel-E-Score Ensemble illustrated to the left.

FOUR IMPORTANT TEL-E-SCORE FEATURES

1. Converts spectators to bowlers.
2. Projects scores on screen—visible to all.
3. Increases sponsor's benefits.
4. Speeds the game—teaches beginners to score.

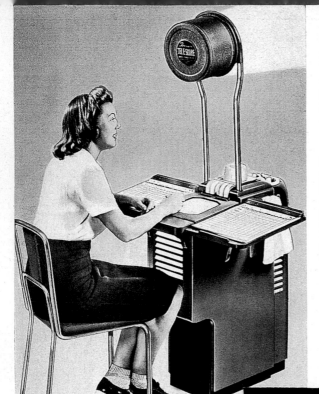

HOW TEL-E-SCORE WORKS

An enlarged image of scores as written on transparent score sheet is projected upon a screen suspended over the approach. Thus, play-by-play scores are clearly visible to bowlers and spectators.

BRUNSWICK EQUIPMENT IS NOW SERVING OUR ARMED FORCES EVERYWHERE

THE *Brunswick*-BALKE-COLLENDER COMPANY
623 SOUTH WABASH AVENUE • CHICAGO 5, ILLINOIS

KEEPING SCORE

Each player bowls two balls in every frame, except when the bowler makes a strike. If a strike is made in the tenth frame, two more balls are bowled. A strike, marked by an "×" in the upper right corner of the frame on the score sheet, is made when the player levels all the pins with the first ball delivered. In this case, a second ball is not bowled. A spare, desig-

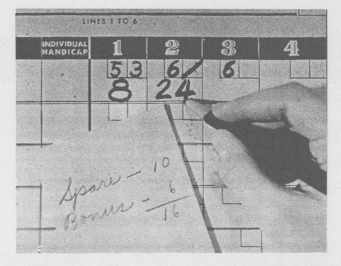

nated as a "/," is made when the player bowls down all the pins after delivering two balls, and, when a spare is made in the tenth frame, another ball can be bowled.

After making a strike, the player is credited with 10 pins plus all the pins made on the next two balls delivered. In the event a second strike is made, another strike symbol is marked, but no figures are written in either of the two frames (the reason for this being that since a strike counts 10 pins plus what pins are scored on the next two balls, no figures can be marked until two balls are rolled following the strike). Two strikes in succession entitle the player to 20 pins in the

frame in which the first strike was made, plus the number of pins bowled down on the first ball delivered in the following or third frame.

If a third successive strike is made, the player is credited with 30 pins in the frame in which the first strike was bowled, while in the second frame he or she would be credited with 20, plus the number of pins bowled down on the first ball delivered in the fourth frame. After making a spare (/), the player is credited with 10 pins plus the pins bowled down on the next (first) ball in the following frame. When neither a strike nor a spare is made, add those pins knocked down to the total in the previous frame.

63

Alley Fashions

DRESSING FOR THE GAME

SNAP, DAZZLE, COOL. POLYESTER, SILK, AND SATIN. WITH THEIR offbeat colors, Main Street affiliations, and eye-popping graphics, bowling alley fashions strike to the core of our style sensibilities. Although every sport has its signature uniform, what makes the sportswear of bowling unique is its unconventional, sometimes chic, frequently retro, and occasionally kitschy synthesis of function and fashion.

Almost without exception, each ensemble is a stand-alone advertisement often personalized with the bowler's name, affiliation, and an icon from bowling folklore or

the sport's hall of fame. For example, shirts may be embroidered with reclining beauties accompanied by the caption, "Opole Bachelors Club," or with the gold vinyl silhouette of a woman's face and hair or with a martini glass filled with bowling balls instead of olives. Humor is usually part of the equation. On one shirt, a roadrunner steaming down the alley like a bowling ball triggers admiration and a giggle. Of course, there is no dearth of groans—"No, no, no! Not a gold spandex shirt with hot-pink trim and purple shoes on a sixty-year-old man!" Wacky slogans, wild colors, and off-the-wall graphics make the bowling shirt come to life. The most original and collectible shirts were manufactured in the 1950s, a decade during which Americans fell in love with big, flashy cars, became hooked on television, and flocked to bowling alleys by the busload.

As important as pattern, color, and imagery were to the unique character of the bowling shirt, they never interfered with function. Bowling a perfect game was always the objective, so it was important that bowling shirts were constructed so they would not compromise the game. Accordingly, the typical cut of a classic bowling shirt included loose tailoring, side and sleeve pleats for easy arm movements, and an open collar. The preferred textiles were also selected for comfort of motion, with gabardines

THE SOLES OF BOWLING SHOES
are made of two materials. One sole
(left) is made of rubber for braking.
The other (right) is made of leather for
sliding. The toe of the rubber sole is
often protected by a leather tip.

being standard for pre-1950s shirts, cotton or rayon in the 1960s, pure polyester in the 1970s, and in the most recent decades, blends of polyester and cotton.

But in bowling, it's the shoes that can either make or break your outfit—and the game. If you've ever rented footwear from a bowling alley, you know that the color of the shoes is guaranteed to clash with what you are wearing. As author and bowler Michael Benson notes in *Essential Bowling*, "If you were looking for some plain black bowling shoes, fuhgeddaboudit! Bowling shoes have generally been available in two styles: colorful and brightly colorful." Because the classic delivery requires a sliding lead foot toward the foul line, possible only if a hard, slippery sole is worn on the sliding foot, bowling shoes are essential. Shoes featuring a rubber heel on the sliding foot, so as not to mark or damage the lane, first appeared in the 1920s.

While bowling without the proper shoes may actually be against lane rules, toting a ball without a bowling bag is downright dangerous. A loose bowling ball spells disaster for anything breakable, especially toes. Bowling bags can control those sorts of pitfalls. And the best part? Unlike large, cumbersome duffel bags, bowling bags are a sensible, streamlined solution.

The earliest bowling bags, from the late nineteenth and early twentieth century, were actually crate-like wooden boxes. Beginning in the 1940s and continuing

The Finest in
Bowling Accessories

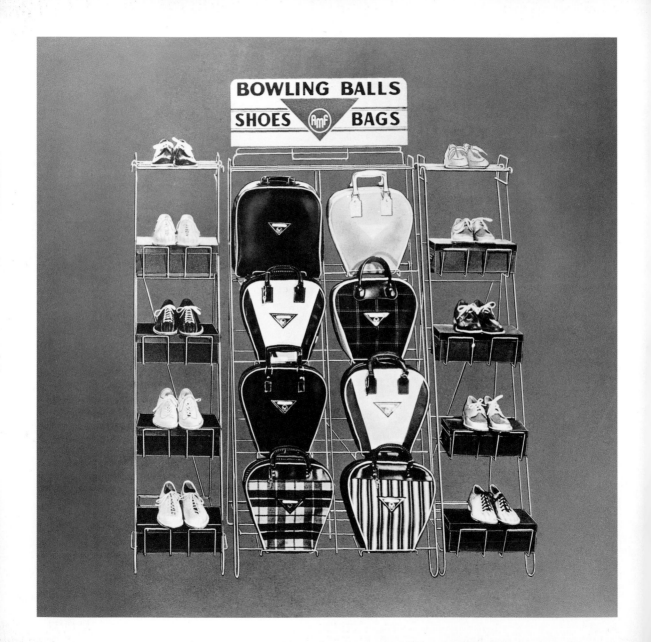

"SUSPEND-O" $2.95
DESIGNED FOR MEN BOWLERS
...by Weber Bowling Shirt Co.
INCLUDES 15 BACK LETTERS AND POCKET NAME
ECONOMICAL - POPULAR - COMFORTABLE
TEAM IDENTIFIER
ON AND OFF IN A JIFFY
SNAP-ON-CLIPS TO TROUSER
. . . NO BUTTONS
YOUR TEAM NAME HERE
Beautifully Embroidered
Your Pocket Name Here
George's Garage
"Bill"
LIMITED SPECIAL OFFER
WEBER'S "SUSPEND-O" at 1/2 PRICE* ($1.50)
WITH SHIRT ORDER
(Send for Free Catalog)
FEATHER-WEIGHT . . . ADJUSTABLE ELASTIC STRAPS
ITEM NO. 100 "SUSPEND-O"
COLORS: GRAY - KELLY GREEN - MAROON
NAVY BLUE - BROWN
ONE SIZE FITS ALL
Any Color Team Lettering Desired.
ORDER YOUR "SUSPEND-O" NOW
OR
SEND FOR CATALOG
OF 19 SMART COLORS IN
MEN'S SHIRTS
AND
WOMEN'S BLOUSES
YOUR CHOICE OF
"PERSPIRATION-PROOF"
SATIN OR WASHABLE
GABARDINE
FRE
1950 PERSONAL SCORE
✓CHECK ONE

These hip-rider pants matched with a peppermint-striped cotton "grand daddy" shirt and sleeveless zip jacket is a bowling fashion as chic as any you will find.

Here's high fashion in bowling in the form of a coral wool jersey dress. The skirt unbuttons to reveal matching pants.

Be certain the bowling clothes you select offer lots of freedom of movement. Skirts should have extra pleats.

Boys' bowling shirts should have a full shoulder, allowing lots of arm action.

STYLE 145

throughout the 1960s, bowling bags were made from softer materials such as canvas or, preferably, leather, and they were either printed or hand tooled with catchy designs. Some of the best bags were ornamented with piping, stitching, and graphic elements that coordinated with shirts.

Mid-century bowling bags and shoes served as a visual notice that the carrier or wearer was a force not to be messed with. Today, of course, the same costume has quite unexpectedly acquired a secondary meaning. A number of haute couture houses have appropriated elements from bowling style, catapulting it from the arena of sport into the theater of fashion. Thus, a retro-style bowling shirt/shoe/bag announces the wearer as a player in the fast game of fashion.

LOW-CUT BOWLING SHOES are comfortable and attractive. They are available in many colors and styles.

Knight, Black
$13.95

Cougar
$12.95

Mojave
$11.95

Rogue, Black-White
$9.95

Lolli-bag, Blueberry
$9.95

Banner, Red-White-Blue
$7.95

Desert
$7.95

Newport
$7.95

Colony-Red
$5.95

Colony-Black
$5.95

Custom LTD
27.95

Tournament
19.95

Executive
14.95

Caravelle, red, also in
avocado and black 13.95

Mustang blue,
also in black 9.95

Torino chianti, also in
charcoal bronze 12.95

Silhouette raspberry
7.95

Silhouette tapestry
7.95

GTO butterscotch
Also in white, red or blue

GTO black

Show your good taste. Choose a color-coordinated Brunswick ball, bag & shoe ensemble.

lolli*pop!
115281
by Brunswick

BOWL-O-BILIA

Between 1910 and 1960, a profusion of paper, plastic, and ceramic ephemera called attention to the delights of the game. Such souvenirs and memorabilia reflected a wide range of artistic sensibilities: Victorian, Art Nouveau, Art Deco, Streamline Moderne. The objects themselves—unpretentious, practical, and cheap—made their way into the pockets, kitchen cupboards, and family game rooms of the sport's aficionados and, as the century neared its close, increasingly migrated into the personal archives of pop historians and collectors of American kitsch.

By means of countless mugs, cups, plates, dishrags, matchbooks, caps, glasses, keychains, and bottle openers, the clubbiness and sociability that bowling alleys fostered spilled over into every facet of life. A team sport deeply rooted in the social network of the workplace, the church, and the family, bowling fostered personal relationships, making way for the importance of the picture postcard. Bowling teams and alley owners mailed photo cards to promote champions, naughty cartoons reminded players that bowling had a steamy underside, and cards with wordplays and silly limericks added a humorous dimension to the popular pastime. Penny postcards explored a number of themes, from the stiff, formal portraits of bowling stars such as

Martin Kern and Emma Jaeger at the beginning of the century to glitzy souvenir postcards from such bowling champions as Gene Gagliardi. Most champions boasted postcard-size publicity photos annotated with their credentials, which bowlers collected as others might baseball or football cards. When budgets permitted, bowling-alley proprietors printed slick, linen-surfaced cards in full color, amusing customers with corny puns, humorous anecdotes, or paeans to the virtues of bowling.

"Keep out of the gutter" was a popular postcard admonition, as was "It strikes me I should write, but it's only now I've had the time to spare." Postcards aimed at women extolled the health virtues of bowling and rallied them to the sport with appeals such as "For Your Figure's Sake!" On the whole, however, most cards leaned toward the humorous, poking fun at a gamut of bowling-alley gaucheries. Heavy on slapstick and visual puns, the cards celebrated the messy vitality of lane life. Cartoons depicting bowlers fanny-down on the lanes were annotated with tag lines such as "When you are down this way, I'd like to see you," or "Now ladies, watch this!"

While the human element in bowling was handled comically, the facilities and

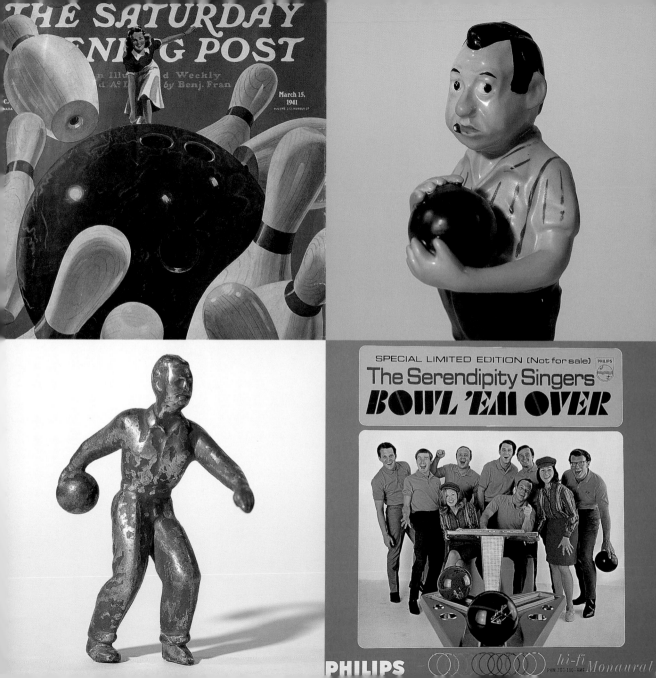

BOWL
in
AIR CONDITIONED
Comfort
COCKTAIL LOUNGE

ow it's Pepsi-for those who think young

re's more action in spare time today...and more Pepsi, too! Light, brac-

PEPSI-COLA

BOWL
for **health**

SPARES **AND** STRIKES
FOREVER **DON CARTE**
WITH CHRIS SCHENK

DON CARTER TELLS
CHRIS SCHENKEL HOW!

LEARNING TO BOWL?
WANT TO IMPROVE
YOUR GAME?

cameo

equipment were given a documentary, often reverential treatment. Full-color picture postcards highlighted snappy details, comfortable appointments, and the spaciousness of bowling establishments. Detail shots of chrome, Naugahyde, and brightly colored amenities lured potential customers. Many cards capitalized on the architectural grandeur of new bowling alleys, with one establishment hyping "corridors built to a king's taste [that] offer a breathtaking spectacle."

In the decades of bowling's heyday, when tobacco was actually advertised as a healthy, status-enhancing accessory of the good life, bowling alleys often promoted themselves on the covers of matchbooks. Colorful imagery and snappy typography touted the social, moral, and physical benefits of the game and lured enthusiasts with lines such as "Bowling's for everyone . . . Bring the whole family" for the Bowling Proprietors' Association of America (BPAA). Some were printed with panoramic elevation drawings of the alley's exterior. Most matchbooks pitched bowling as a complete entertainment package, relying on comforts such as air-conditioning, cocktail lounges, restaurants, "streamlined alleys," and fully automated pinspotting.

In the 1950s, an avalanche of bowling knickknacks, diplomas, toys, and household objects rolled off assembly lines and printing presses at home and abroad. American bowlers just couldn't seem to get enough of award patches, board games, dishware, and stationery utensils emblazoned with bowling's signature icons. Ashtrays, known for their "gutter" humor, bore inscriptions such as "Old bowlers never die, their balls end up in the gutter." Toy manufacturers produced bowling board games. For example, "Tenpin Alley," developed in the 1930s, required threading a miniature ball through a "strike zone gate" along a foot-long board. Whether kitschy or tasteful, cheap or expensive, bowling-inspired ephemera was a part of the game, promoting and celebrating America's passion for what had once been deemed the "game of kings."

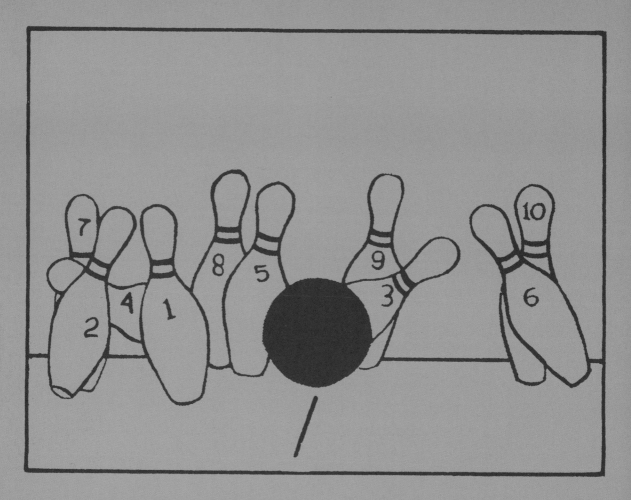

Pins "Topple"—Correct

Pins "Fly"—Incorrect

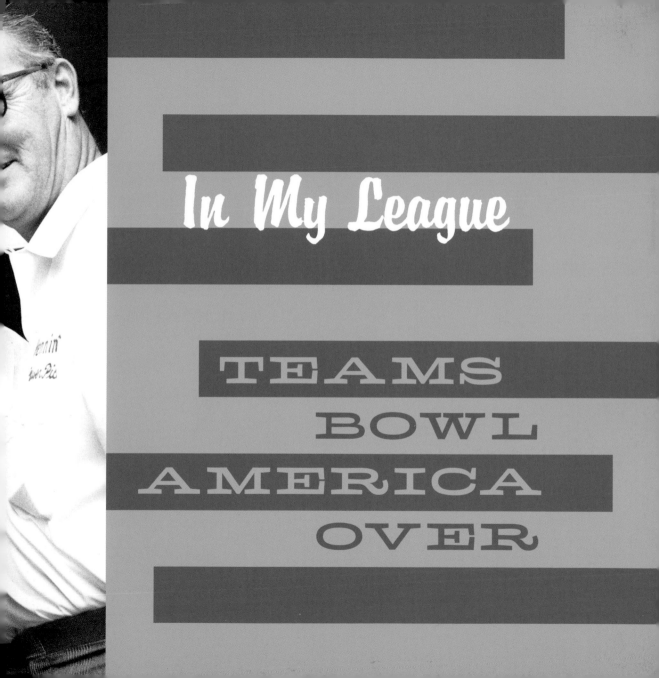

In My League

TEAMS
BOWL
AMERICA
OVER

"TO BOWL OR TO BOOZE?"—THAT WAS THE QUESTION. ALTHOUGH
bootlegging was rampant during the 1920s, in that era it was no longer possible to get a drink at a bowling alley, a development that radically changed the nature of the sport and its client base. To compensate for major losses in alcohol sales, alley proprietors cleaned up their establishments and wooed families with their "dry alleys,"

emphasizing the virtues of the sport for spirit, mind, and body. Even *The Journal of the American Medical Association* reported that "physicians recommend bowling, for it exercises unused muscles of the body and can be played year-round."

With the repeal of Prohibition in 1933, alley proprietors faced a difficult decision. They could reinstate the saloon ambience that had nurtured the sport during the early part of the century, or, by maintaining wholesome, alcohol-free, family-oriented venues, they could continue to cultivate enthusiasm among the thousands of women and younger players who had taken up the sport during the "Dry Years." Because both options offered opportunities to increase profits, proprietors took the middle road of combining bowling and beer into the "Double-B Guarantee" that would catapult the sport into an unprecedented era of popularity and profitability.

Breweries that were emerging from the "Dry Ages" in the middle and late 1930s had their own interest in supporting bowling. They wanted to reinsert themselves into the economy and explored how they might do so by exploiting some of the old, pre-Prohibition venues. A good part of their effort also involved some fundamental "image" revamping that would disassociate beer and drinking from its criminal reputation. A number of breweries struck up collaborations with bowling alleys to create environments that struck an acceptable balance between the mildly raucous delights of social alcohol consumption and the down-to-earth pleasures of family and

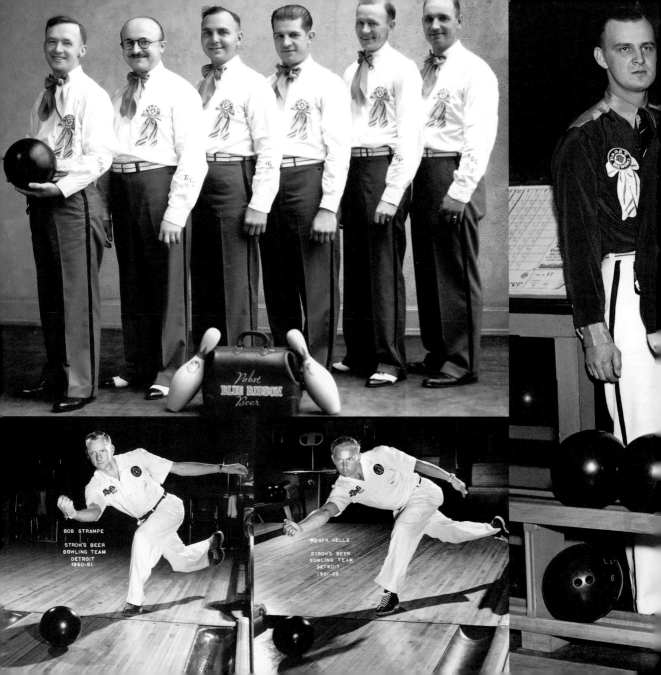

BOB STRAMPE
STROH'S BEER
BOWLING TEAM
DETROIT
1960-61

ROGER HELLE
STROH'S BEER
BOWLING TEAM
DETROIT
1961-62

Meister Bräu
"THE BEER"

league bowling. They subsidized the sport by offering free instruction and special promotions—such as reduced game fees, tournament prizes, special competitions—in alleys that served beer, as well as overhauled interiors to make them attractive to families. Even such minor aesthetic touches as fresh paint on the walls, the addition of curtains, soundproofing, and good lighting paid rich dividends in a significant increase in casual, recreational play, and eventually, tournament and league play for women and children.

Although the number of Americans participating in "open-play bowling" rose dramatically as lanes became automated—and more attractive—proprietors preferred to see their lanes filled with leagues, which guaranteed them a steady flow of customers and games. Along with those for men, the growing number of tournaments and leagues for women and kids sanctioned by the Women's International Bowling Congress and the American Junior Bowling Congress helped solidify the sport's base of support.

Attracting women to the sport had always been a key part of expanding the appeal of bowling. After the war, to make up for the decline in women's industrial-league bowling, alley owners changed their approach. Rather than pitching their appeals to large corporations, they organized merchants' leagues around retailers that catered primarily to women. The strategy worked; the postwar period saw the emergence of new "ladies' leagues" composed of teams sponsored by florists, jewelers, sportswear stores, and other establishments targeting a predominantly female market. In fact, when it comes right down to it, the frame-by-frame story of how league play came to dominate the game reads like a Madison Avenue passion play, complete with pitchmen, promotions, and promises.

After World War II, establishments relied even more heavily on industrial leagues to populate their alleys than they had in the preceding decades. Taking the long view, proprietors encouraged companies that had sponsored teams in the previous year to renew their contracts. If there were still slots to be filled in the tournament calendar, proprietors solicited interest among nearby firms, usually approaching plant managers, to whom they would extol the benefits of a recreation program anchored to bowling. For their part, industrialists and small business owners came to see plant-sponsored bowling as a way of improving relations both among workers and between workers and management.

On occasion, however, the political and social virtues attributed to bowling leagues strained the limits of credibility. For example, Brunswick, the bowling manufacturer, advised proprietors to let executives know that a corporate-sponsored league not only contributed to goodwill among employees but also alleviated tensions by giving "department heads and employees, both men and women, a chance to meet on an equal basis and develop an understanding of each other's problems." A number of corporations bought into this philosophy hook, lane, and sinker. Hulburt Smith, the president of L. C. Smith & Corona Typewriters, indicated in a company brochure that he had organized five leagues so his employees might get to "know each other in a friendly way." Meanwhile, at the Fashion Park–Stein Bloch Corporation in Rochester, New York, executives supported worker bowling leagues to smooth relations between the front-office staff and factory workers. Determining exactly how well these strategies actually worked is up to specialists in labor history. But, judging from the swelling popularity of the game, the proliferation of bowling alleys, and the burgeoning of organized competition that cut across class lines, it would appear that the game's benefits extended far beyond the walls of the bowling emporia.

For all their utopian objectives, the architects of the factory–bowling alley alliance failed to make room for one segment of the labor force in their schemes for social harmony. African Americans, Asian Americans, and Native Americans were

systematically excluded from participation in bowling leagues and even from admission to bowling alleys. This color discrimination was a relatively new phenomenon in a sport that, so long as it was confined to the saloon, knew no color barriers. As bowling moved out of the saloon in the 1920s and 1930s and became more competitive, it also became more segregated. Both the American Bowling Congress and the Women's International Bowling Congress, as well as, in the 1940s, the American Junior Bowling Congress, explicitly barred people of color from the competitions they sponsored. After World War II, however, the situation began to improve as the National Negro Bowling Association began to attract support and help from organized labor. In 1947, the United Autoworkers threatened to withdraw their sponsorship of leagues and tournaments that excluded minorities, and the following year the International Ladies' Garment Union followed suit. Under pressure of legal action, the American Bowling Congress finally agreed to integrate competition in 1950, though another decade would pass before racial segregation within bowling alleys, leagues, and tournaments was on its way out.

Most bowlers were drawn to organized bowling for personal reasons—status and gain. The monetary rewards for competing successfully at various levels were not insignificant. And, even though it was relegated to a marginal position in comparison to its earlier prominence, betting still yielded a modest fiscal incentive to play. The appeal of cash prizes drew bowlers to regularly scheduled sweepstake tournaments. For the modest investment of a $25 entry fee, a player could return to the plant with winnings as high as $2,500, no small reward for the pleasure of bowling.

If league bowlers were more concerned with boosting their incomes, keeping their uniforms spotless, and posing for endearing team photos and celebrity shots, others saw the rise of league bowling as the ultimate antidote to the "red scare." The editor of a New York City bowling newsletter went so far as to suggest that bowling was an important bulwark of defense against the development of radical ideology among workers. He noted that "no bowlers ever turn Communist," because the sport simply took up too much time and energy that might otherwise be devoted to the consideration of dangerous Marxist doctrines. And just in case a factory worker was tempted by "Moscow ideals," bringing workers and foremen together in a bowling league would surely "be the end of any feeling of class consciousness." The theory certainly worked for bowling proprietors, who derived about 50 percent of their revenues from league play during the 1950s.

Money, politics, and convivial social intercourse aside, league players were attracted to alleys that captured the razzmatazz spirit of the times. The sharp increase in the number of leagues between 1934 and 1956 went hand-in-hand with the renovation of scruffy, multileveled bowling parlors into snazzy, ultramodern entertainment centers outfitted with sleek metal, glass, and plastic furnishings. As Howard Stallings explains in *The Big Book of Bowling*, "the glossy, hard ball speeding down a super-slick, blonde, wooden surface, smashing into mathematically arranged, streamlined pins, meshed perfectly with the era's 'need for speed,' the aerodynamic *zeitgeist*, if you will." And when Ozzie and Harriet, Bob Hope, and Jerry Lewis picked up bowling balls, it was clear the game had fully become part of the American dream.

With league play and family-oriented bowling firmly entrenched, the bowling industry had succeeded in putting the ultimate "spin" on the sport. Who would have thought the game's hard-pressed impresarios, in a matter of only twenty years, could have transformed a simple if tawdry pastime for down-on-their-luck roughnecks into a mainstream pursuit that took on utopian connotations?

In the 1950s, repositioning bowling as a recreational activity appropriate for the entire family required not only a fundamental rethinking of the game's infrastructure—its location, setting, and facilities—but a retooling of human behavior. If the game were to attract respectable, clean-living folk, proprietors realized, moving it from shabby, marginal locales into sparkling, hygienic facilities would only be part of the solution. Solving the rest of the problem would require transposing the manners of the drawing room into what had largely been a rough-and-tumble bastion of manly camaraderie. To this end, bowling associations from the local to the national levels began to append guides to bowling etiquette to their rulebooks, and bowling alley operators posted lists of behavioral do's and don'ts where their patrons would be sure to see them. *Politeness* and *timeliness* were the operative words. Team bowlers were encouraged to arrive at the lanes punctually. If anything should detain them or prevent them from coming, they were to communicate with their team captain so that a substitute could be arranged. As in driving, so in bowling, players observed certain fundamental "rules of the bowl." For example, when two bowlers on adjoining lanes are rolling first balls, or each one is bowling at a spare, the bowler on the right has the "honor" to proceed.

Team spirit is always advocated to prevent ruffled feathers and foul tempers. "Just as in football or baseball, a good sport congratulates his opponent on his strikes and good conversions," advises *The Etiquette of Bowling*. "It is highly improper to 'needle' an opponent or an opposing team with taunts or comments on misses or splits." Every bowling etiquette expert warned that exhibitions of temper or complaints about alley conditions or "luck" were in terribly bad taste.

Bowlers also should never offer "free advice" to other bowlers unless explicitly asked to do so. One of the top bowling teams in the country enforced a strict rule that warned team members against making any suggestions to each other without the express permission of the team captain, which, incidentally, was given only in the most extreme cases. "The reason for this rule, which should be observed by all team bowlers, is that the bowler who is bowling badly becomes more confused than ever when criticism or suggestion for correction is offered. The best advice, if advice must be given, is 'Take your time,' which really is more of a psychological correction, good no matter what he is doing wrong."

Don't needle an opponent while he's making his shot.

Give priority to the man on your right.

Don't use someone else's ball without permission.

The Bowl
of Fame

PIN
YOUR
HOPES
ON ME

From left:

WHITEY HARRIS

RAY BLUTH

DICK WEBER

PAT PATTERSON

DON CARTER

TOM HENNESSEY

WHOLESOME, EARNEST, AND REFLECTING THEIR WORKING-CLASS origins, the game's high rollers have demonstrated that dedication and hard work can take you a long way. The game's most notable stars—Hank Marino, Don Carter, Andy Varipapa, LaVerne Haverly, and Marion Ladewig—are to be admired not only for hitting strikes with uncanny consistency, but for leading decent lives and for putting a premium on friendship, family, and good citizenship.

The majority of mid-century bowling legends rose to prominence while still employed in manual trades. For the most part, they were rugged, strong-jawed, and strong-willed working-class men. Few bowlers had more colorful stories—or more successful careers—than such alley greats as Hank Marino and Andy Varipapa. Their involvement in the bowling world at the turn of the century highlights the role that the sport played in urban immigrant communities as an engine for social advancement, a source of ethnic pride, and, without contradiction, the path to assimilation.

Born in Palermo, Italy, Hank Marino made his way to the United States at the age of ten. Marino worked in his brother's barbershop until he opened his own seven-chair haircutting parlor at the age of fifteen. By the early 1900s, Chicago had emerged as a bowling hot spot, and Marino took up the sport as his primary form of recreation. A long string of victories at national and international tournaments in the 1920s and 1930s gained him the distinction of being the nation's top bowler, earned him a spot in the Bowling Hall of Fame, and the honor of being "Bowler of the Half-Century," so designated by the National Bowling Writers Association.

Another Italian immigrant with a place in the Hall of Fame is Andy Varipapa. The ball-handling virtuoso's biography begins like Hank Marino's, but veers off in a slightly different direction—like one of Varipapa's trick shots. Varipapa emigrated from Italy at the age of ten, and settled in Brooklyn, New York. He got a job at a foundry that made door hinges, and almost every day after work, he'd head off to an

No. 410C

No. 410B

No. 410A

No. L1X

No. L2X

No. L3X

No. 991

No. 990

No. D53F

P3
P3
P3

alley to bowl. By studying the more accomplished bowlers, Varipapa refined his skills and developed a knack for performing trick shots. He could throw a boomerang ball that would reverse direction halfway down the lane and spin back to the foul line, and he could even knock a pin into the air and have it topple another pin in an adjoining lane! His most celebrated stunt involved converting the difficult seven-ten split by rolling two balls consecutively from either side of the lane at different speeds so that they crossed paths and knocked down the two standing pins at the same moment. These shenanigans landed Varipapa movie deals and cross-country publicity tours and helped him earn his celebrity status. But after World War II, Varipapa got serious and began to concentrate on developing his legitimate bowling skills for formal tournament play. The effort rewarded him with two consecutive all-star national championships in 1946 and 1947, making him the first two-in-a-row winner and, of course, securing him a place in the ABC Bowling Hall of Fame.

But the "highest and holiest" bowler of them all was Don Carter, who dominated bowling during its heyday in the 1950s. He was to bowling what Michael Jordan was to basketball, and he is considered by many to be the greatest bowler who ever lived. As Andrew Hurley explains in *Diners, Bowling Alleys, and Trailer Parks*, "The 'St. Louis Shuffler,' so called due to Carter's unorthodox crouching approach to the line and his bent-elbow delivery, racked up the most impressive career statistics in history." He won four all-star championships, six Professional Bowler's Association (PBA) championships, five World's Invitational titles, the ABC Masters, and was named Bowler of the Year six times. His success earned him a million-dollar contract—he was the first athlete ever to sign one—with Ebonite, to promote their bowling equipment.

Meanwhile, champion LaVerne Haverly, one of the game's most celebrated women bowlers, shocked the straightlaced fans by flaunting her sexuality and competitive aggression. In fact, few players in the game's history rocked the foundations of the sport more than Haverly in the course of her bowling career from the early 1950s well into the 1970s. She was known as the "blonde bombshell," according to *Bowling Magazine*, ". . . for the way she has thrown pin-fans throughout the country into a tantrum." In one competition with male bowler "Clown Prince" Calder, Haverly was simply too hot to handle. Calder raised the stakes to a full-fledged war between the sexes, saying, "No blonde or brunette or even a redhead is gonna beat a man of my stature. It's still a man's world." In his dreams. Haverly bested him in six out of seven matches.

While Haverly was bowling's fiery vixen champion, Marion Ladewig was its most famous grandmother. In 1963, the 48-year-old grandmother of five and member of the Brunswick advisory staff won the third World's Invitational tournament of her career. She was honored by the Helms Foundation as Michigan's Woman Athlete of All Time and was named "Woman Bowler of the Year" seven times, not to mention the seven National Match Game titles in which she carried the Brunswick banner.

With bowling heroes making a media splash, the sport was given another boost into the mainstream when Harry Truman installed lanes in the White House in 1947, and was widely photographed in classic bowling poses. Surely there was no greater tribute to the sport's respectability than the image of a homegrown-boy-made-good hooking the presidential ball. Small wonder, then, that the iconic figure of the bowler represented America's most cherished virtues, as was demonstrated in 1948, when *Life* magazine published a Rockwell-esque portrait of America's bowlers. "Once a week a timorous shoe clerk can . . . put on a brightly colored shirt, rub chalk on his hands, and face up to the pins. And on that unforgettable night when he pulls his team out of a hole with three strikes in the tenth frame, he really becomes an Andy Varipapa."

Murray Johnston Drennon Felt Robe

Leave It to Lyle

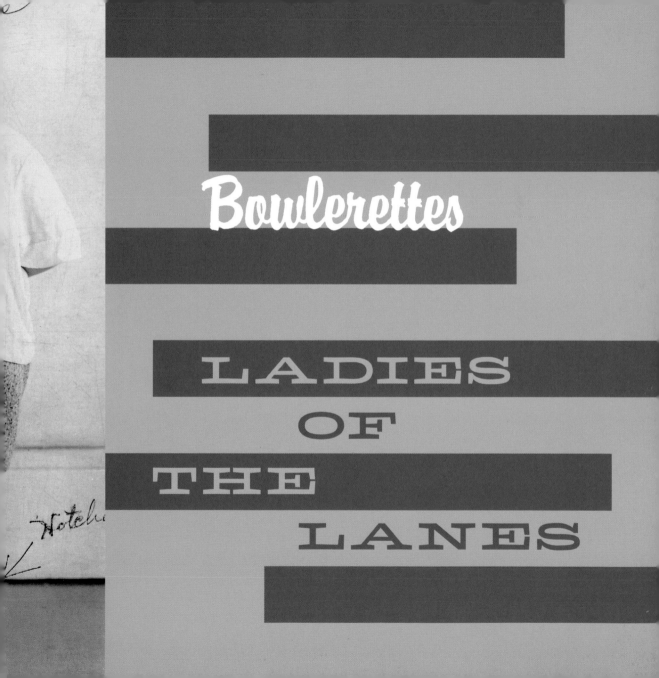

South St. Louis Dairy Co. - 1945

KAY DAUMIT ～ LUSTRE CREME
1944 ～ Champions ～ 1945

15"

5"

BY THE MID-TWENTIETH CENTURY, MEN HAD BEEN BOWLING FOR decades. Women, on the other hand, looked back on a somewhat spotty history in the bowling alley that ranged from total exclusion during the male-dominated "saloon years" to domination during World War II, when their men had gone off to fight. After the war, many women found themselves with free time during the day, when bowling lanes tended to be vacant. With men unavailable to bowl during the afternoon, alley owners realized that women were prime candidates for keeping the lanes humming. Proprietors, seeing a golden opportunity, moved quickly to mechanize their lanes to rid them of jeering pinboys who kept women and novice bowlers away from the game.

The strategy succeeded beyond the proprietors' wildest expectations. By the 1940s, ladies' bowling had attained the dimensions of a veritable craze. With pride and conviction, the editor of a 1947 issue of *The Woman Bowler* congratulated the "bowlerette" of the 1940s for being not only an athlete, but also a "woman of action," who, even while keeping abreast of the "latest coiffure," was involved in "the activities of her community, her city, and yes, her nation."

Leading manufacturers were now motivated to develop gender-specific equipment, competitions, and promotions, which drew tens of thousands of women to the sport. Brunswick launched the "Lady Brunswick" line of lighter balls for women, with the Whelanite available in mottled patterns of "cornflower blue" and "explosive pink." Brunswick's "Junior Mineralite" ball, weighing only eight pounds, was a hit among both women and children. In 1957, the John E. Sjostrom Company of Philadelphia manufactured a series of lightweight and mid-weight bowling balls that weighed in at nine, eleven, twelve, and thirteen pounds.

Because many women were starting families during the postwar era, convenient access to alleys was a must. Market-driven proprietors opened lanes in suburban shopping centers specifically with an eye to drawing in women on shopping excursions. **115**

Campaigns designed to get women bowling enlisted the cooperation of retailers, who distributed flyers that announced free bowling instructions, free coffee, and most important, free nursery services. One of the key objectives in this marketing strategy was to make women comfortable about leaving the home and to reassure them that they would not be neglecting their parental responsibilities while engaging in recreational pursuits. With this in mind, virtually all of the bowling centers built in the 1950s incorporated nurseries. Most of them kept matrons on duty and offered youngsters a variety of amusements: popper-rollers, building blocks, plastic telephones, and hobbyhorses. And because alley owners were always on the lookout for future customers, miniature plastic bowling sets were de rigueur.

The bowling industry sought to fill the social void created by the flight to the suburbs and positioned itself as the refuge of the disconnected. Proprietors understood that to entice women into bowling alleys they had to also persuade husbands to allow their wives to bowl. This was accomplished by explaining at length the various benefits of the bowling break. Typically, publicists played on a husband's sense of guilt about his wife's entrapment in daily activities that provided little or no variety in the day-to-day routine, and precious little incentive to keep up her appearance.

Finally, in bowling, as in all other areas of life, there is nothing like sex to make a sale. It seems that the bowling spin-doctors knew no shame when it came to making extravagant claims about how throwing a ball at a bunch of wooden pins could inject excitement into a marriage. That is exactly what they did in magazines, newspapers, radio, and industry newsletters. An article in *The National Bowlers Journal and Billiard Revue*, for example, explained that even when a husband and wife bowl on separate teams, bowling enhances marital bliss because the shared avocation helps "hubby and wife" develop a "deeper understanding" of one another.

On a Roll Again

THE
GAME
GOES
COSMIC

IN TODAY'S AGE OF MEDIA HYPE
and sports overkill, the time-honored
game of bowling, with its populist origins
and grassroots enthusiasm, is unique
among sports. Embracing the young and
old, the rich and poor, and casting a wide
net over aficionados both urban and suburban, bowling has for years rolled along
in its friendly, unassuming fashion—a sport of unchallenged integrity.
With its accessibility and offbeat sense of humor, bowling remains an
entertaining and curious part of American culture and a colorful
reminder of the rewards and enjoyment sports can provide for all
segments of society.

After its collapse in the 1960s, bowling faded from the spotlight
for at least two decades while America's attention turned to basketball and football. But in the late 1990s, popular interest in bowling hit
an upswing. Now, with the construction of some spectacular bowling
centers and bowling attire's appearance in the world of high fashion,
the sport is no longer thought of as a pastime reserved for families
and/or the middle-aged.

In recent years, bowling-alley proprietors introduced new features designed to attract the younger clientele such as multicolored
halogen spotlights, sophisticated sound systems, overhead screens with
automated, computerized scoring, and extensive food concessions.
New architecture transformed the outdated look of the 1960s and 1970s
with airy, eye-popping postmodern structures and stressed the "total

entertainment" nature of bowling centers. Grand, brightly illuminated glass-brick atria and pulsating, wildly colored neon lights invited bowlers into a "mall" environment. Reflecting the high-tech aesthetic that had infiltrated the arenas of commerce and other sports, bowling alleys installed state-of-the-art equipment in scoring programming, computer game analysis, and electronics. To further expand their appeal, some centers incorporated miniature golf, video-game arcades, and swimming pools as part of the entertainment menu.

Most recently, the game has gone "cosmic." Usually offered after eleven P.M., cosmic bowling has gained the endorsement of both parents and teens. Although the rules of the game are the same, in cosmic bowling, the alley is completely transformed. Black lights are used to illuminate the bowling center, so that pins and balls glow as they move through space. Television screens play nonstop music videos, and loud dance music completes the cosmic atmosphere. The writing is on the ball. All signs are that the humble sport of bowling has struck a new chord in the hearts of the wild and restless.

BIBLIOGRAPHY

Banes, Ford. *Right Down Your Alley.* N.p:
A.S. Barnes & Co., 1946.

Bellisimo, Lou, and Larry L. Neal. *Bowling.*
Englewood Cliffs, NJ: Prentice-Hall, Inc.,
1971.

Benson, Michael. *Essential Bowling.* New
York: The Lyons Press, 2000.

Clause, Frank. *How to Win at Bowling.* New
York: Fleet Publishing Co., 1961.

Dulles, Foster Rhea. *A History of Recreation:
America Learns to Play.* New York:
Appleton-Century Crofts, 1960.

Fraley, Oscar. *The Complete Handbook of
Bowling.* Englewood Cliffs, N.J.:
Prentice-Hall, Inc., 1958.

Heise, Jack. *How You Can Bowl Better Using
Self-Hypnosis.* Hollywood, CA: Wilshire
Book Co., 1968.

Hurley, Andrew. *Diners, Bowling Alleys, and
Trailer Parks: Chasing the American
Dream in Postwar Consumer Culture.*
New York: Basic Books, 2001.

Kalman, Victor, ed. *AMF Guide to Natural
Bowling.* New York: Permabooks, 1961.

Kogan, Rick. *Brunswick: The Story of an
American Company from 1845 to 1985.*
Skokie: Brunswick Corporation, 1985.

Miller, Mark. *The Bowlers Encyclopedia.* 4th
Edition. Greendale, WI: Bowling
Headquarters, 2000.

Riess, Steven A. *City Games: The Evolution
of American Society and the Rise of
Sports.* Urbana, IL: University of Illinois
Press, 1989.

Sayrs, Hank. *The How-to Book of Bowling.*
New York: Fawcett Publications, 1962.

Stallings, Howard. *The Big Book of Bowling.*
Salt Lake City: Gibbs Smith, 1995.

Taylor, Dawson. *The Secret of Bowling
Strikes!* No. Hollywood, CA: Wilshire
Book Co., 1960.

Tonelli, Joe, and Marc Luers. *Bowling Shirts.*
Atglen, PA: Schiffler Publishing Ltd., 1998.

Weiskopf, Herman. *The Perfect Game: The
World of Bowling.* Englewood Cliffs, N.J.:
Rutledge Books, 1978.

Wene, Sylvia. *The Woman's Bowling Guide.*
New York: Mokay Co., 1959.

ACKNOWLEDGMENTS

This book required the professional services of many talented, enthusiastic, and knowledgeable individuals whose love for bowling and literature is in perfect game territory. Those who deserve special recognition include Travis Boley, director of the Bowling Archives at the International Bowling Museum and Hall of Fame, and Linda Travis, assistant director, both of whom provided invaluable services, consultation, and direction. We are especially grateful to St. Louis photographer Linda Wilson, who produced impeccable and beautiful images of primary source material from the Bowling Museum; all the photographs of three-dimensional bowling memorabilia, ephemera, and bowling fashions that appear in this work represent her enlightened eye and professional capabilities.

We would also like to acknowledge a number of friends and family who provided source material, personal anecdotes, and materials that helped give life to the project. In this regard, Amy Ault, a Harrisburg bowling enthusiast and humorist, provided important clippings, books, and artifacts about bowling. David Culverwell contributed important analyses of the modern day bowling phenomenon. Katrina Lenček-Inagaki provided editorial commentary and professor-cum-cultural historian Lena Lenček provided brilliant insights into the significance and semiotics of bowling in modern times.

Finally, we would like to acknowledge our editors at Chronicle Books, who conceived the idea for this book in the first place, and then stood with us every step along the way, providing expert editorial commentary, a crystalline vision for what shape this book should take, and creative talents in the area of book design. We are grateful to Benjamin Shaykin, a bowling aficionado, for his inspired designs, layouts, and picture selection. Our copy editor, Jacqueline Volin, provided perspicacious commentary and pruning of our prose.

Every book has its luminaries behind the scenes, and in this regard, most of all we'd like to thank our hard-working, always inspiring, and extremely talented editors, Leslie Jonath and Jodi Davis. Through every phase of the project, they provided brilliant counsel, they offered specific and timely suggestions that demonstrated an unshakable commitment to the project, and most important, they imparted their cool taste and forward vision to every dimension of the book, from words and images to organization and ideas. An author couldn't ask for more.

—*Gideon Bosker and Bianca Lenček-Bosker*

GIDEON BOSKER is an award-winning author and cultural historian whose interests range from bowling, barbecue, and beaches to wallpaper, fabrics, and mid-century design. He is the co-author of *Beaches*, *Atomic Cocktails*, *Patio Daddy-O*, *Fabulous Fabrics of the 50s*, *Greetings From the French Riviera Postcards*, and *Highballs High Heels*, all published by Chronicle Books.

BIANCA LENČEK-BOSKER is an avid observer of and participant in the world of popular culture. A collector of vintage perfume bottles and an accomplished equestrian, she prefers to bowl to a good beat wearing glittery shoes. This is her first book.

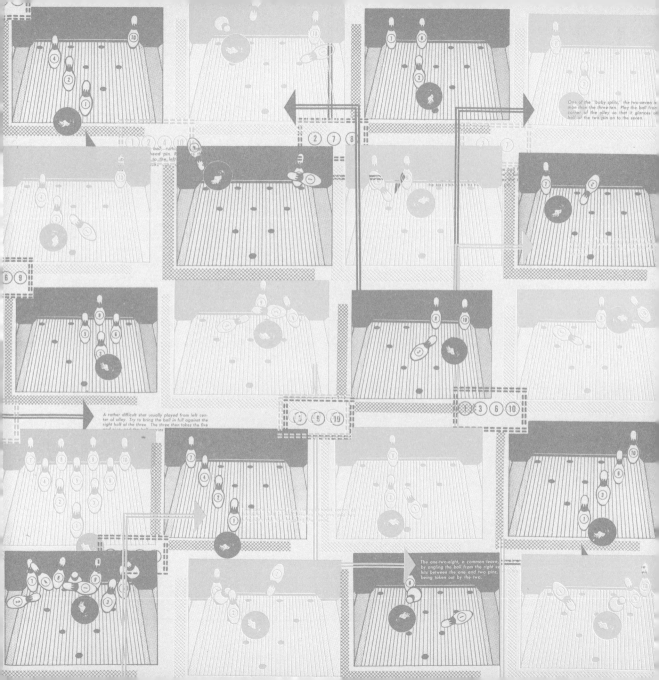

One of the "baby splits," the two-seven is more than the three-ten. Play the ball from corner of the alley so that it glances off half of the two pin on to the seven

② ⑦ ⑧

⑥ ⑨

A rather difficult shot usually played from left center of alley. Try to bring the ball in half against the right half of the three. The three then takes the five and half the two carries

③ ⑨ ⑩

① ③ ⑥ ⑩

The one-two-eight, a common leave, by angling the ball from the right hits between the one and two pins, being taken out by the two.

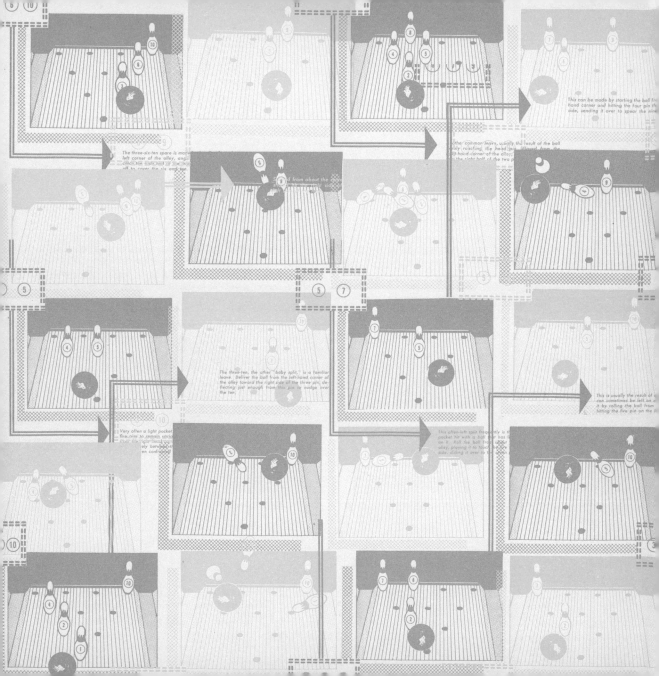